W9-DJP-674

CONTEMPORARY WRITERS IN CHRISTIAN PERSPECTIVE
A CONTINUING SERIES EDITED BY RODERICK JELLEMA

Ernest Hemingway

A CRITICAL ESSAY
BY NATHAN A. SCOTT, JR.

WILLIAM B. EERDMANS / PUBLISHER

The quotations from various works of Ernest Hemingway that appear
in this booklet are protected by copyright and have been reprinted
here by special permission of Charles Scribner's Sons.

TO

Robert and Margaret Grant — Bob and Peggy —
Souvenir of a decade's friendship

NATHAN A. SCOTT, JR. is a graduate of the University of Michigan (A.B., 1944), Union Theological Seminary (B.D., 1946), and Columbia University (Ph.D., 1949). He holds honorary degrees from Ripon College (Litt.D.) and Wittenberg University (L.H.D.). Since 1955 Dr. Scott has taught in the Divinity School of the University of Chicago, where he presently serves as Professor of Theology and Literature and Chairman of the Theology and Literature Field. He is also a Fellow of the School of Letters of Indiana University.

Dr. Scott, who is a priest of the Episcopal Church, is co-Editor of *The Journal of Religion* and Book Review Editor of *The Christian Scholar.* His most recent book is *The Broken Center: Studies in the Theological Horizon of Modern Literature* (Yale University Press, 1966). Among his other books are *Modern Literature and the Religious Frontier* (1958), *Albert Camus* (1962), *The New Orpheus: Essays Toward a Christian Poetic* (1964), *The Climate of Faith in Modern Literature* (1964), and *Samuel Beckett* (1965). He has also contributed essays to fourteen symposia, and a large body of articles to literary, philosophical, and theological journals in this country and abroad.

It was in a religiously desperate moment of the last century that Matthew Arnold was led to embrace his doctrine of the "touchstone." For, having lived through a time in which the foundations of the *fides perennis* appeared to have been destroyed by the new biology of Darwin and the new biblical criticism of Continental scholarship, he did at last feel bound to conclude that not a creed was unshaken, that not an accredited dogma was by way of escaping the general dissolution, and that to Humane Letters alone could man still look for the guidance and salvation that had once been sought in formal religion. So, since poetic literature had now to assume the ultimate burden, of bracing the human spirit against whatever shocks it might be heir to, it seemed manifestly to have become the case, as Arnold insisted, that "the best poetry" could alone be tolerated. And thus the great task of criticism became that of raiding the history of literature for little golden nuggets of "high . . . truth and seriousness," and then of applying these nuggets as norms, as "touchstones," in the ascertainment of the "true rank" of books and authors. For, if literature were to be counted on for the saving of our souls, it clearly was of the highest importance that the wheat be judiciously separated from the chaff.

But if, as I suspect, other possibilities for securing man's ultimate peace can be descried, then we shall have no need to impose on literature so great a burden as Arnold wanted it to assume. And thus we shall also have no need to fidget, as he did, over matters of "rank." Indeed, the handing out of grades with plus and minus marks seems always, finally, to be a sterile business of special pleading and pontification, and I have no confidence in it. What, for example, would be the profit, the real profit, in ranking Ernest Hemingway in relation, say, to D. H. Lawrence and Thomas Mann and André Malraux and Vladimir Nabokov and Samuel Beckett? Such an exercise can no doubt be performed, but it is one for which I cannot summon any very high interest, for Henry James was grappling,

I believe, with the essential truth about the artist, when he had the writer Dencombe declare on his deathbed (in the story called "The Middle Years"): " 'We work in the dark — we do what we can — we give what we have. Our doubt is our passion, and our passion is our task.' "

And surely the great thing is that Hemingway, working perhaps in the dark and doing only what he could, did, nevertheless — in finding his passion in his doubt and in making that passion his central task — create a literature that has been read with a consuming interest for forty years, and one by which we have ourselves been read in a way unparalleled by many other bodies of writing in this century. He is, in short — simply as a fact of the spiritual history of our period — *one* of the great ones, whatever may be the "true rank" that they will be assigned by some Final Arbiter. And the pressure of his career is felt as a lively force today, whenever and wherever men take thought of the principal writers of the age, for *In Unserer Zeit* and *Og Solen Gar Sin Gang* and *L'Adieu aux Armes* and *Morte nel Pomeriggio* and *El Viejo y el Mar* and *A Moveable Feast* belong to the international tradition of modern literature.

A part of the pressure that Hemingway exerts upon us is, of course, undoubtedly an affair of the personal myth, and the Legend that a highly stylized life gathered around itself. The early years have, I suppose, no especial interest. He was born on the twenty-first of July in the closing year of the last century in that western suburb of Chicago called Oak Park, less splendid than the suburbs to the north of the city, on the Lake front, but a quietly respectable community solidly rooted in the bourgeois decorums, where his father was a prosperous physician and his mother, though presiding over a family of six children, managed also to be a pillar of local religious and musical enterprises. The father had a great appetite for the outdoor life, for hunting and fishing and exploration, and thus the family spent their summers in the north woods of Michigan, where, at Horton's Bay near Petoskey, Ernest learned early to relish and master the disciplines and rituals of life in the open air, winning the prowess as hunter and fisherman in which he was to take a lifelong pride. And, at home, he was boxing in Chicago gymnasiums and playing on the football and basketball and baseball and track teams of Oak Park High

School, in every way being more influenced apparently by his father's avocational interests than by his mother's.

Yet, despite what seems on the surface to have been the carefree ease of this comfortable middle-class boyhood, there were obscure tensions in the relation with both his father and his mother, leading to his twice running away from home for brief periods. And in the autumn of 1917, after having been graduated from high school the previous spring, he went to Kansas City, where the experience that he had gathered on the staff of his high school newspaper enabled him to land an appointment as a cub reporter on the *Star*. As he was to say many years later, "I wanted to work on the *Star*, because I thought it was the best paper in the U.S." But, war having broken out, he also wanted to get overseas, and, in the spring of 1918, he enlisted with the Red Cross as an ambulance driver, for service on the northern Italian front. And it was there, at Fossalta di Piave, on the 8th of July, 1918, while distributing chocolate to Italian troops, that shrapnel from an Austrian mortar tore into his legs and shattered his right knee cap. Yet, even so, though under constant gun fire, he managed to carry a wounded Italian soldier several hundred feet to a dugout shelter — for which he was subsequently decorated by the Italians. By October, after several operations on his knee, he had recovered sufficiently, however, to enter the Italian infantry, in one of whose élite units he fought until the Armistice.

In the spring of 1919, he returned to Oak Park, but remained only for a short time, going on from there to Toronto to work on the *Daily Star* — but then returning to Chicago in the autumn of 1920, where he stayed until the following year when, after his marriage to Hadley Richardson of St. Louis, he went back to Toronto with his bride in September, becoming a few months later a foreign correspondent for the *Star*, with special assignment to the Greco-Turkish War. But during this period his commitment to a literary vocation was steadily deepening, and, by the winter of 1922, he and Hadley had settled into a little Paris apartment near the Place du Tertre, and, having already found his way into the circle of Anglo-American expatriate-writers in the city (Gertrude Stein, Ezra Pound, John Dos Passos, Ford Madox Ford, Archibald MacLeish, James Joyce, Scott Fitzgerald, *et al*), he was busily at work on stories

7

— and, shortly, on a first novel. In the summer of 1923, Robert McAlmon, the head of the Contact Publishing Company in Paris, published Hemingway's first book — *Three Stories and Ten Poems;* in the spring of the following year the journalist William Bird, who was publishing on an old hand press handsome small editions of little books in Paris under the imprint of the Three Mountains Press, brought out a collection of sketches entitled *in our time;* and, with the New York publication by Boni and Liveright on the 5th of October, 1925, of the collection of stories, *In Our Time* (the inter-chapters of which were comprised of the sketches issued by the Three Mountains Press), the years of apprenticeship were over, and one of the great literary careers of the century had been launched.

This first American edition of *In Our Time* (numbering only 1335 copies) did not, to be sure, make any great stir, so that Horace Liveright was disinclined to accept Hemingway's second book, *The Torrents of Spring*, most especially since it was a novel (about a Harvard esthete and his involvements with the native yokels in a northern Michigan town) that was most maliciously parodying the style of Sherwood Anderson, who was then Liveright's most valuable literary property: indeed, Liveright did quite flatly reject the book, thus in effect releasing Hemingway from any further legal obligation to deal with the firm. And it was then that Scribner's editor, Maxwell Perkins, having been earlier led by Scott Fitzgerald to take an interest in Hemingway, was free to bring him into the Scribner stable: *The Torrents of Spring* was immediately accepted, and was published in May of 1926. But, though Perkins had taken on a shoddily written and an utterly meretricious piece of frivolity that Hemingway had turned out in little more than a week's time in November of 1925, he had, as a result, established this young man on the Scribner list and had thereby won the rights to the remarkable book that he published only five months after the release of *The Torrents — The Sun Also Rises,* which was an immediate success and which made Hemingway famous before his twenty-eighth birthday. In the following year the collection of stories, *Men Without Women,* appeared; and, at the end of the 'twenties, there came the great popular triumph of *A Farewell to Arms,* of which, within four months after its appearance in September of 1929, nearly eighty thousand copies had been sold, giving Hemingway his first large success in the market of the country's bookstores.

It was in the following decade, as the burdens of fame settled down upon him and he moved through a succession of marriages (to Pauline Pfeiffer and to the writer, Martha Gellhorn — both, like Hadley Richardson, of St. Louis), that the Hemingway Legend began to grow. Throughout these years the man was intensely involved in the practice of his craft: it is, to be sure, only the novel on the Spanish tragedy written at the end of the 'thirties and published in 1940, *For Whom the Bell Tolls,* that bears unmistakably the marks of major accomplishment, and just as unmistakably is the book of 1937, *To Have and Have Not,* a thoroughly bad piece of work. But, nevertheless, when one thinks also of the book on bullfighting of 1932, *Death in the Afternoon,* and the collection of stories, *Winner Take Nothing* (1933), and the brilliant account in *The Green Hills of Africa* (1935) of his hunting-experience in Tanganyika and the publication in 1938 of *The Fifth Column and the First Forty-Nine Stories* — when one thinks of this whole body of work, it is apparent that the 1930's were a period in Hemingway's life of sustained and very considerable labor. Yet what seems to have most caught the public's attention during this period was the "glamor" of the hard-drinking, chest-thumping, wisecracking, handsomely grinning sportsman and athlete who boxed in the ring with professionals, who hunted lions in the African bush and bighorn antelope in the wild country of Wyoming and Montana, who caught giant marlin and tuna from his fishing boat, the *Pilar,* in the Bahamas and the Florida Keys, who donated ambulances and supplies to the Loyalists in the Spanish War and went to Spain as a correspondent for the North American Newspaper Alliance — and whose photographs, as a consequence, were regularly to be seen in the Sunday Supplements, picturing him on some perilous frontier of sport or war looking (as Edmund Wilson noted) very much like Clark Gable. And, with the advent of the IInd War, this image of Hemingway was even further enlarged by his cruises for the Navy off the Cuban coast in the *Pilar,* by his participation as a foreign correspondent in missions of the RAF, and by his spectacular adventures in combat with the Fourth Division of the First Army in Luxembourg and at Hürtgen Forest.

In the years after the War, he published only two books — that embarrassing disaster which appeared in 1950, *Across the River and into the Trees,* and then, two years later, the utterly beautiful and profoundly moving novella about the heroic struggle of an old Cuban fisherman to bring a giant marlin back from the Gulf Stream, *The Old Man and the Sea.* These were years of relatively quiet happiness, spent with his fourth wife, Mary Welsh, chiefly at their farmhouse, *Finca Vigia,* in the little town of San Francisco de Paula, a few miles outside Havana, and, at the last, at their lodge in Ketchum, Idaho — though there were frequent trips to old haunts on the Riviera, in Paris and Venice, in Spain and Africa. But, even during these years, there were periodic occurrences that disclosed the continuing power of the Legend to charm the popular imagination — as when, for example, after his second plane crash in Uganda in January of 1954 and it was believed he was dead, the rumor (in point of fact quite false) quickly spread that, when he did appear, he emerged from the jungle with a bottle of gin in one hand and a cluster of bananas in the other. So, at the end, as both body and spirit were severely battered by all the various blows absorbed through more than forty years of hazard, it was widely felt that the design of the life had found its natural completion on that morning — the second of July, 1961 — when, feeling all the vitalities of earlier years to be irretrievably gone and not wanting to die with any of the messiness he had always despised, the old man destroyed himself with a twelve-gauge shotgun in his lodge at Ketchum.

It was a life — as it had been lived in extreme situations of stress, with consummate energy and bravado — that for forty years had given the young everywhere (in America, in France, in Italy, even in Russia) an example of militancy and valor, and of a zest for the human adventure that, to a remarkable extent, seemed untainted by any motive of self-protective prudence. So — like André Malraux and Antoine de Saint-Exupéry — Hemingway belongs amongst those writers of our time whose personal myth competes with their work for our attention, and, as I say, the pressure of the Legend continues today very strongly to be felt.

But the greater part — and the really significant part — of that pressure which I have spoken of his exerting upon us has to do surely not with the Legend but with the vision which his art communicates of what is ultimately man's situation in the world, of its challenge and peril, and yet of the clouds of glory that overhang the earth with the promise that it shall abide forever. As Alfred Kazin remarked a few years ago, his final effect as an artist "was to leave people with a distinct moral attitude" — it was to leave people with a sense of the radical holiness of the world and of the gift of life itself, and with a confidence in the possibility of transcendence, of man's being able at last to prevail, if a right course can be kept with sufficient scrupulousness and integrity.

What is powerfully bracing and affirmative in Hemingway's rendering of the human story has, of course, often gone unrecognized by those who could discern only the harsh surfaces of his fiction. They have noticed how frequently the iconography and ritual of war and crime and sexual promiscuity and death figure in the novels and stories, how repeatedly the personages of the fiction inhabit a lawless and brutal world, how doggedly their lives are shadowed by defeat and ruin, how generally the characteristic human situation seems to be an affair of desperateness and fearful risk — and so it is concluded that the vein being mined is that of a violent naturalism "bent on proving," as Van Wyck Brooks said, "that life is a dark little pocket." Brooks's judgment (in *The Opinions of Oliver Allston*) was handed down, it is true, twenty-five years ago, at a time when Hemingway's achievement had not been submitted to so careful an assessment as it has received in the intervening period: but, nearly fifteen years after Brooks's philippic, even so sensitive a critic as Professor Leon Edel of New York University (in an article in *Folio*) was claiming to find a similar crudity in the fiction, and such a biliousness of perspective continues on occasion to be expressed.

Now the only way, it seems to me, in which the literature can be released from the injustice of this kind of hostility is by our simply making a return to the texts themselves and permitting them to settle the issue. And when, just about fifteen years ago, I was by way of cross-questioning myself out of an earlier indifference and beginning to work towards a fresh view of Hemingway's art, it was a comment of Lionel Trilling's which suggested a new angle of approach: but it was not so much a line of argument as simply a word that he used in talking about Hemingway and Faulkner in an essay in *The Liberal Imagination* — it was his choice of a single word that suddenly had the effect of focalizing what I had obscurely been feeling to be a central element in *The Sun Also Rises* and *For Whom the Bell Tolls* and many of the stories, and that very shortly was to announce itself even more emphatically in *The Old Man and the Sea* as a decisive ingredient of Hemingway's vision. Mr. Trilling was wanting to remark the extent to which the writers of this century with whom we have the most "active, reciprocal relationship" — amongst whom he was including Hemingway and Faulkner, along with a number of Europeans — are men who stand rather markedly apart from, and even occasionally somewhat explicitly against, that general secular ambiance surrounding the culture of "liberal democracy." And, in the case of Hemingway and Faulkner, the word which he chose to specify this element of recalcitrance was "piety." "It is," he said, " a word that I have chosen with some care and despite the pejorative meanings that nowadays adhere to it, for I wished to avoid the word 'religion,' and piety is not religion, yet I wished too to have religion come to mind as it inevitably must when piety is mentioned." And it was, he suggested, their implication in a certain body of pieties — not necessarily descending in any direct and immediate way from a formal religious tradition — that established the remove at which these two American writers stood from many of the characteristic assumptions about human life that are sponsored by the secular mentality of liberal democracy.

This was, to be sure, an idea which Mr. Trilling broached only in a very tenuous and allusive way: yet immediately the mere conjoining of the notion of piety, in however loose and undeveloped a fashion, with Hemingway's vision of the world had the effect of confirming me in what I had long been feeling to be very much at the center of that vision. I had, for example, always been deeply moved by a certain scene in *For Whom the Bell Tolls* — which, more and more, had struck me as having a profoundly exemplary character in Hemingway's fiction, the kind of quality, say, that might have led Erich

12

Auerbach to use the episode as the whole basis for his discussion of Hemingway, had he ever undertaken to discuss great "scenes from American literature" in the manner of his treatment of European tradition in *Mimesis*. And the scene in the book on the Spanish War that I have in mind is that of Robert Jordan's death.

At the end the young American's mission is completed. From the Escorial, a few miles northwest of Madrid, he had been sent into the Guadarrama mountains to blow up a bridge — which would be the signal for the attack on Segovia. And now, after four difficult days of work and planning, the bridge has been destroyed. But on this last morning the little band of guerrillas who have been his accomplices are very nearly wiped out altogether by the Fascist planes overhead: the only survivors are Pablo, the leader of the band, his wife Pilar, Primitivo, Agustín, and Maria, the lovely crop-headed girl between whom and Jordan an intense love affair has developed during their days together in the Guadarramas: only these are left. Yet they, it seems, now that the bridge is blown, will make good their escape into the forest and on to a place of safety, with the horses that have been kept waiting. But, just as they are preparing to leave the place of sabotage which is a dangerously exposed slope above the bridge, Jordan's leg is fractured by a shell from an enemy machine-gun. And immediately it is apparent to Pilar and the others, as well as to Jordan, that now he cannot travel and that the *Inglés* must therefore be left behind — which means that he must be left alone to die. " '*Anda*,' he said to [Pilar]. 'Go.' " And Pilar turns away, "with her head down without saying anything nor looking back and Robert Jordan could see her shoulders shaking." Maria begs to be allowed to remain with her adored Roberto and has forcibly to be taken away. " 'Nay, rabbit,' " says Jordan. " 'What I do now I do alone. I could not do it well with thee. . . . But if thou goest then I go with thee. It is in that way that I go too. . . . There is no good-by, *guapa*, because we are not apart. . . . Go now.' " Pilar and Agustín, with great affection, bid him farewell. " '*Salud, Inglés*.' " " '*Salud*,' " he answers. Then, taking the girl Maria, they wheel their horses round and, with grief in their hearts, ride quickly out of sight.

"They were all gone now and he was alone with his back

13

against a tree." Alone and about to die: and this last hour of Jordan's makes, I believe, one of the great scenes in modern fiction, and one which is, I submit, empowered by a certain quality that will be found to be deeply a part of what may well be most characteristic of Hemingway's account of the human reality.

"They will be coming soon now, he thought." The time is short, and the Fascist cavalry will soon be bursting through the timbered curtain of the environing woods. "You have had much luck," he says to himself. "There are many worse things than this. Every one has to do this, one day or another. You are not afraid of it once you know you have to do it, are you? No, he said, truly." So, given the inevitable, he faces into it with a stern poise and dignity, being comforted by the thought that "the world is a fine place and worth fighting for. . . ." And it is to the *world* that he bids farewell. "He looked down the hill slope again and he thought. I hate to leave it, is all. I hate to leave it very much. . . ." But leave it he must: so, in a spirit of reverent affection, he *looks* at the nearby stream, and again at the hillside and at the pines. "Then he looked up at the sky. There were the big white clouds in it." And, at last, as he sees the cavalry begin to ride up the slope — "He touched the palm of his hand against the pine needles where he lay and he touched the bark of the pine trunk that he lay behind." And having *touched* the good earth in a final act of homage, he lies back and rests as easily as the raging pain of his leg will allow, to await the end.

Now I submit that it is Mr. Trilling's word which most accurately renders what we are moved by in this scene, for that which is being acted out by the man who is about to die is a profound piety — toward the earth and the beautiful, unstrident simplicity of its persisting presence. Like the Camus of *Noces* and *L'Été,* the hero of *For Whom the Bell Tolls,* one could say, is sustained in the last great emergency of his life by the "loving alliance," by the "simple accord," between himself and the glorious fecundity of the world, its sights and smells and sounds and tactilities. And, as he rests in his final hour against the pine needle floor of an Iberian forest, he makes us feel, as he *touches* the soil beneath him and *looks* at the sky overhead, that he is prepared to declare with the Camus of *Noces* that "if

14

there is a sin against life, it is perhaps not so much in despairing as in hoping for another life, and in concealing the implacable grandeur of this one." It is true, of course, that on the night before the exploding of the bridge he had, for the merest moment, remembered his father's suicide and had inwardly conceded that "Anyone has a right to do it. . . ." "But," he thought, "it isn't a good thing to do. I understand it, but I do not approve of it. . . . You have to be awfully occupied with yourself to do a thing like that." And, in his own last extremity, it is not with himself he wants to be solely occupied: but, rather, what he attempts to do is to perform an act of lucid attention before the great enchantments of the earth, and what this wounded, dying man surrenders to is "the happy lassitude of my nuptials with the world" *(Noces)*. He exchanges (in Camus' words) "the smile of complicity" with the happy smile of the sky and the forest and a running brook in the Guadarrama mountains, and it is this profound sense of intimacy with mute, insensate things that helps him to die well, as it had also helped him to live well. In some such way as this, it seems, he is enabled (in the language of Paul Tillich) to experience "the power of being . . . even in face of the most radical manifestation of nonbeing."

So, remembering the Wordsworth whose habit it was to address hymns of praise to "Fountains, Meadows, Hills and Groves," to "rocks, and stones, and trees" and stars, and to salute the sunshine's "glorious birth," we can speak perhaps of a Wordsworthian element in Hemingway's novel on the Spanish War. But it is to be found not only there but also throughout his entire work, appearing and reappearing as a persistently recurrent attestation to a kind of biological faith in the ultimate power even of "the meanest flower that blows" to bring peace to the human heart. Indeed, it is the Wordsworthian element in Hemingway that has often caused his fiction to put me in mind of one of the most famous passages in the literature of Reformation Christianity. The Westminster Catechism, it will be recalled, opens with the great question: "What is the chief end of man?" And there follows the equally great answer: "To glorify God and enjoy him forever!" Thus it was that the doctors of seventeenth-century Presbyterianism wanted to begin their catechizing of the faithful. And it was, one feels,

15

a fine instinct of theirs that led them to confront the catechumen, at the very beginning, with a question that reaches back to levels of sensibility and awareness antedating anything belonging distinctively to the Christian dispensation. For neither the idea of glory nor the idea that it is to be enjoyed speaks of what our duties to God entail or of how He enters the world and deals with humankind: but, rather, they speak of that most primitive dimension of our encounter with religious reality in which we are laid hold of by what Rudolph Otto called the *mysterium tremendum et fascinosum* and thus invited to contemplate and to enjoy (in the spirit of E. E. Cummings) "this amazing/day . . . the leaping greenly spirits of trees/and a blue true dream of sky . . . and . . . everything/which is natural which is infinite which is yes." The glory is that surplusage of meaning in the ordinary, everyday realities of the world that lifts the mind above its own horizon to contemplate the beauty and stability and permanence of Creation: it is that ontological amplitude wherewith the things of earth elicit a radical kind of astonishment at the "miracles which are daily with us" in the water we drink, in the bread and fruit that we eat, in the blossoming of trees and the mysteries of vegetation, and in all the bounties that make the human enterprise possible. The glory is the imperial majesty with which life flourishes and is renewed and *lasts,* and, as Wordsworth understood more profoundly than any other poet of the English language, it is the distinctive privilege of man to enjoy it.

Now I say it is a Wordsworthian kind of piety that consistently figures as a leitmotif — running, to be sure, at times *against* certain other motifs — in all of Hemingway's work. It is, indeed, to be felt in his earliest writing, and with particular force in the Nick Adams stories which were brought together in the book of 1925, *In Our Time.* It was Philip Young who suggested several years ago in his fine book on Hemingway that the title *In Our Time* might be an allusion to that sentence in the versicles of the Anglican Prayerbook's Evening Office which says, "Give peace in our time, O Lord." And, if this be so, then we may regard such a story as "Big Two-Hearted River" as indicating the kind of peace which Hemingway's book envisages.

The story is divided into a Ist and IInd Part which, together, comprise the last two chapters of the book. By this point, in the narrative of Nick's growing up which is formed by the preceding stories, he is a young man who has been abroad and who has fought and been injured in the War. But it is not only his body, it seems, that was bruised by the war experience, for, like Frederick Henry later in *A Farewell to Arms,* he too, being seared deeply by the ordeal, contracted for himself a "separate peace." And now, just beneath the surface, there is much that would indicate that, midway the journey of this life, he is lost in a dark night: so, since it is "a long time since Nick had looked into a stream and seen trout," he returns to the Michigan woods for his fishing expedition, in a spirit of delighted anticipation of the joys ahead and of relief at putting an unmastered and troubling world behind. After getting off his train in a little hamlet that he discovers now to have been burned out a year earlier, he finds, as he moves off into the country toward his camping site, that the summer heat makes hard work of walking up-hill and carrying his pack — but, even so, he feels happy: "He felt he had left everything behind. . . . It was all back of him." And when he grows tired, he slips his pack off and lies down under the shade of an island of pine trees. "His neck and back and the small of his back rested as he stretched. The earth felt good against his back."

At last towards evening, deep in the back country, near that point of the river which he wants to work for trout, he selects a level piece of ground overlooking the water for his camp-site and pitches his tent. This is an operation which he performs with great care and competence — the smoothing of the ground, the pegging of the canvas, the arranging of cheese cloth across the open mouth of the tent to keep out the mosquitoes. And, when the tent is finally up, he crawls into it to arrange his provisions. "He was settled. Nothing could touch him. . . . He was there, in the good place." And it is this sense of being *in the good place* — by a clear, cold trout stream and in the midst of the north woods — that gives to the entire story its beautifully soothing Arcadianism. Nick's gathering of grasshoppers for bait, his making of fires and his frying of his food over the flames, his wading in the trout streams, and his casting for the fish — all this is enacted as if

17

it were a loving ritual of cleansing and communion and celebration. When he catches a trout, he pulls it to the surface
of the water, tenderly unhooking the barb from its mouth and
dropping it back into the water. And he is careful not to touch
it before wetting his hand, because he remembers that, when
it is touched with a dry hand, a white fungus attacks the un-
protected spot. Then he sits "on the logs, smoking, drying in
the sun, the sun warm on his back, the river shallow ahead
entering the woods, curving into the woods, shallows, light
glittering, big water-smooth rocks, cedars along the bank and
white birches, the logs warm in the sun, smooth to sit on,
without bark, gray to the touch" — and we know that, whatever may have been the cause of that malaise of spirit into
which this young man had somewhere been driven, he is now
once more on the way to felicity and peace, having been
touched by the healing power of the good earth. And he
evidently himself begins to be conscious of this, for, as we are
told, "He did not want to rush his sensations any."

And, just as the Wordsworthian element shows itself early on
in the progress of Hemingway's literature, it is also to be dis-
cerned in the late work as well. In, for example, *The Old Man
and the Sea,* surely a part of what it is that wrenches the heart
so profoundly is a quality in old Santiago deeply akin to that
reverent piety toward the radical holiness of the world which,
nearly thirty years earlier, had made young Nick Adams so
engaging a figure. It is something which Carlos Baker spotted
in his book on Hemingway and which, with his characteristic
exactness of definition, Professor Baker spoke of as the old
fisherman's spirit of "gallantry" toward all the creatures of the
sea and the air. Santiago knows that his livelihood depends
upon his catching fish, and he takes this for granted: he is not
a foolish sentimentalist, and, had he ever heard of Dr. Schweitz-
er's doctrine of "reverence for life," it would doubtless have
struck him as a silly kind of fastidiousness and as a luxury
which he could not afford. But, though he must kill, he has
a great respect for his antagonists, and even a sense of brother-
hood with them: once he hooks the great marlin, for example,
and the long struggle begins, he thinks towards midnight: "We
are joined together and have been since noon. And no one
to help either of us." And, even as he beseeches the Holy

18

Mother to "pray for the death of this fish," he adds — "Wonderful though he is." Nor is this tough, gaunt little man without a loving compassion for all the unhoused and more delicate forms of seafaring life "that bide the pelting" of the ocean's cruel whims. "He was very fond of flying fish" and "was sorry for the birds, especially the small delicate dark terns that were always flying and looking and almost never finding, and he thought, 'The birds have a harder life than we do except for the robber birds and the heavy strong ones. Why did they make birds so delicate and fine as those sea swallows when the ocean can be so cruel. . . . Such birds that fly, dipping and hunting, with their small sad voices are made too delicately for the sea.' " And we are told that, after he hooks the great marlin, he pities him, though his sorrow never relaxes his determination to kill him: he pities him in his wounded, massive dignity and pain: he thinks to himself, "Never have I seen a greater, or more beautiful, or a calmer or more noble thing than you, brother." And he is " 'glad we do not have to kill the stars.' " In short, the story that is told here makes us feel that it is a celebration, among other things, of the profound solidarity (as Professor Baker calls it) that exists between man and the whole stretch of Creation and that affords a kind of sanction for the belief that the sun and the moon, the dews and the frosts, the nights and the days, the mountains and the hills, the seas and the floods, and all the things of earth "uttereth speech" and "sheweth knowledge" and are exalted forever.

The world, as it is rendered in Hemingway's fiction is, then, a world that is touched by glory — and a certain kind of piety becomes, therefore, a basic norm of human life. But it is a glory that is, as it were, *unexplained,* for it is fully countered by its opposite, in the power of blackness, the blackness which (as Melville said of Hawthorne's) is "ten times black." And Hemingway does in many respects stand very near the center of that tradition in modern literature which is prepared, in effect, to testify — again, with Melville — that, "though in many of its aspects this visible world seems formed in love, the invisible spheres were formed in fright." Like the Conrad of *The Secret Agent* and the Kafka of *The Trial* and the Moravia

19

of *The Time of Indifference* and the Camus of *The Stranger,* Hemingway situates the representative personages of his fiction in — to take a phrase from Camus' *The Myth of Sisyphus* — "a universe suddenly emptied of illusion and light," where every type of consolatory trenscendentalism appears to have lost its persuasiveness and cogency. But he is also like these artists in feeling, as Conrad once remarked, that what is "so hopelessly barren in declared pessimism is just its arrogance." So, unlike, say, the Hardy of *Jude* or the Dreiser of *Jennie Gerhardt* — but in very much the manner of *The Trial* or of Camus' *The Plague* — Hemingway does not give himself to vague, showy speculations about Truth and about the terrible Enigma Behind It All: his characteristic manner is, rather, one of close-lipped reticence and reserve, and he has no great penchant for the rhetoric of metaphysical nihilism. But, nevertheless, a "blackness, ten times black," is there, in the fiction — and a powerful expression of it is to be found in one of his most famous short pieces, the story in *Winner Take Nothing* (1933) called "A Clean, Well-Lighted Place."

The clean, well-lighted place is a Spanish café on the terrace of which an old man sits drinking brandy late one evening, as the two waiters look on from within and talk about their patron.

> "Last week he tried to commit suicide," one waiter said.
> "Why?"
> "He was in despair."
> "What about?"
> "Nothing."
> "How do you know it was nothing?"
> "He has plenty of money."

Then the old man whose despair is unassuagable by money or by any of the largesse normally adjudged by the world as good fortune calls for another drink. And then he calls for still another. But, this time, the younger waiter who is eager to close up for the night and get home to his wife refuses to serve him. His partner, after the old man's departure, asks him, with a touch of masculine irony, if he is not a little apprehensive about getting home before the hour at which his wife usually expects him, but the young husband says, "No. . . . I have confidence."

20

"You have youth, confidence, and a job," the older waiter said. "You have everything."

"And what do you lack?"

"Everything but work."

" 'I am of those who like to stay late at the café,' " says the older waiter. " 'With all those who do not want to go to bed. With all those who need a light for the night.' "

The younger man, though, being full of confidence, is given no purchase in his own experience on what his elder colleague is getting at: so the older man patiently explains that this café where they work is a clean and attractive place, pleasant and well-lighted, and he is always reluctant to close up, he says, simply " 'because there may be some one who needs the café,' " who needs the comfort of its cleanliness and light. And, after the younger waiter has bade him goodnight, he thinks to himself, as he darkens the café and prepares to leave, that his own need for a light in the night is prompted not by anxiety about any particular or specific thing.

> It was not fear or dread. It was a nothing that he knew too well. It was all a nothing and a man was nothing too. It was only that and light was all it needed and a certain cleanness and order. Some lived in it and never felt it but he knew it all was nada y pues nada y nada y pues nada. Our nada who art in nada, nada be thy name thy kingdom nada thy will be nada in nada as it is in nada. Give us this nada our daily nada and nada us our nada as we nada our nadas and nada us not into nada but deliver us from nada; pues nada. Hail nothing full of nothing, nothing is with thee. He smiled. . . . Now, without thinking further, he would go home to his room. He would lie in the bed and finally, with daylight, he would go to sleep. After all, he said to himself, it is probably only insomnia. Many must have it.

Now it is this blackness beyond a clean, well-lighted place — this "nothing full of nothing" that destroys "confidence," that murders sleep, that makes the having of plenty of money a fact of no consequence at all — it is this blackness, ten times black, that constitutes the basic metaphysical situation in Hemingway's fiction and that makes the human enterprise something very much like a huddling about a campfire beyond which looms the unchartable wilderness, the great Nada. And it can, I think, be said that the principal presupposition guiding Hemingway's performance as a writer is the assumption that the reality with which the artist is properly engaged is that of the

21

campfire, for it is the campfire — in its sequestered isolation, in its marooned desolateness — which is felt to be the essential human reality.

Indeed, it is just this determining slant of Hemingway's vision that establishes the fundamental character of his moralism. For, everywhere in his fiction, one senses an obsession with the importance of behaving well — around the campfire. And what is entailed here is at once an ethic of conduct (which is mimetically developed in the dramatic situations of the novels and stories) and an ethic of style, for the artist himself.

The style is, of course, universally recognized today as one of the important innovations of twentieth-century literature and as itself one of the great responses of that literature to an age of war and homelessness and broken faith. And it is in his role as stylist that Hemingway has been felt to be one of the principal *directeurs de conscience* for a generation whose wise men often say, in effect (with Yeats):

> Things fall apart; the center cannot hold;
> Mere anarchy is loosed upon the world.

Indeed, the style is now so famous and so familiar a way of dealing with modern experience that, at this late date, no extensive description of it is necessary. It is a prose, suffice it to say — aggressively colloquial and nonliterary in its rhythms and textures — whose great intention is to get straight "the facts of the matter." Typically, the sentences are short and declarative, the usual limit of syntactical complexity being the statement which is compounded of two independent clauses yoked together by a conjunction. As the late Joseph Warren Beach once remarked, it is a style "with no legato, no holding over of the effect with the blurring of the pedal": it resists whatever might hint of fanciness and "fine" writing: everything must have edge, must be kept lean and stripped and simple, for the style wants rigorously to avoid any strategem of diction or syntax that might have the effect of interposing intrusive qualifications and refinements between the reader and the immediate actuality which he is being invited to contemplate. It is a style that does not want to reach beneath the surfaces of things but which wants, rather, to restrict itself to the bare statement of this-and-that-and-this-and-that: the trick,

22

as Hemingway felt and often said, was to get the thing "the way it was."

As he said of his early newspaper experience in the book on bullfighting of 1932, *Death in the Afternoon*: "In writing for a newspaper, you told what happened, and with one trick or another, you communicated the emotion aided by the element of timeliness which gives a certain emotion to any account of something that has happened on that day. But the real thing, the sequence of motion and fact which made the emotion and which would be as valid in a year or ten years or, with luck and if you stated it purely enough, always, was beyond me and I was working very hard to get it." But already, when he came to the writing of *In Our Time,* he had found what was to become his characteristic way of catching the right "sequence of motion and fact" — as in, for example, the following passage in "Big Two-Hearted River":

> He came down a hillside covered with stumps into a meadow. At the edge of the meadow flowed the river. Nick was glad to get to the river. He walked upstream through the meadow. His trousers were soaked with the dew as he walked. After the hot day, the dew had come quickly and heavily. The river made no sound. It was too fast and smooth. At the edge of the meadow, before he mounted to a piece of high ground to make camp, Nick looked down the river at the trout rising. They were rising to insects come from the swamp on the other side of the stream when the sun went down. The trout jumped out of water to take them.

Or here, again, is a passage bearing the same signature, from that section of *The Sun Also Rises* which is devoted to the journey of Jake Barnes and Bill Gorton by bus from Pamplona to Burguete:

> The bus climbed steadily up the road. The country was barren and rocks stuck up through the clay. There was no grass beside the road. Looking back we could see the country spread out below. Far back the fields were squares of green and brown on the hillsides. Making the horizon were the brown mountains. They were strangely shaped. As we climbed higher the horizon kept changing. As the bus ground slowly up the road we could see other mountains coming up in the south. Then the road came over the crest, flattened out and went into a forest. It was a forest of cork oaks, and the sun came through the trees in patches, and there were cattle grazing back in the trees. We went through the forest and the road came out and turned along a rise of land, and out ahead of us was a rolling green plain, with dark mountains beyond it. These were not like the brown, heat-baked mountains we had left behind. These were wooded and there

23

were clouds coming down from them. The green plain stretched off. It was cut by fences and the white of the road showed through the trunks of a double line of trees that crossed the plain toward the north. As we came to the edge of the rise we saw the red roofs and white houses of Burguete ahead strung out on the plain, and away off on the shoulder of the first dark mountain was the gray metal-sheathed roof of the monastery of Roncevalles.

One sentence gives you a fact, and the next another, and the next another; and they curtly move along, with a kind of terse telegraphy that stabs out at you with a remarkable power. It is a language whose poised and chilly laconicism suggests the impassiveness with which the great looming blackness just beyond the human campfire needs to be faced, if the self-containment which is the mark of man's dignity is not to be surrendered. When the writer insists on simply being attentive to what happens, on simply looking and noticing and reporting, on simply getting the thing "the way it was," "with nothing that will go bad afterwards," it is his way of suggesting, through his own practice as an artist, how one ought to behave around the campfire. As Philip Young has remarked, "The intense simplicity of the prose is a means by which the man says, Things must be *made* simple, or I am lost. . . ." You need to learn to look at the world straight and "true," Hemingway is saying — with no glossing of the facts, and with no grumbling — if you are to learn to confront the truth of your own precarious human existence. The "economy" of the language says you had better not take on more than you can really manage. And the style is "tense," as Professor Young reminds us, "because that is the atmosphere in which the struggle for control takes place, and the tension expresses the fact."

But Hemingway's moralism is expressed not only in his own style as an artist but also in the strict discipline of conduct to which he holds the people of his fiction accountable. And, at the level of manners, this is a discipline which is an exact analogue of that which is regarded as guaranteeing the writer's own integrity. Mark Schorer (in his widely known essay, "Technique as Discovery") has called it a "morality of the stiff lip," and Hemingway himself described it as "grace under pressure" — and either formula can serve as an admirable summary of that ideal of honor and code of conduct in which the controlling

24

ethical norms of Hemingway's fiction are lodged. Edmund Wilson (in *The Wound and the Bow*) named the decisive principle here as one of "sportsmanship" — which suggests, perhaps in a more immediate way, the actual quality of the virtues and vices that the fiction brings into play. For it is indeed something like the discipline of the sportsman which is held up as emblematic of how a man ought to behave. Rinaldi and Frederick Henry in *A Farewell to Arms;* Harry Morgan in *To Have and Have Not;* Robert Jordan in *For Whom the Bell Tolls;* Santiago in *The Old Man and the Sea;* Wilson the hunter in "The Short Happy Life of Francis Macomber"; Jack, the old prizefighter, in "Fifty Grand"; the old matador, Manuel, in "The Undefeated"; Colonel Richard Cantwell in *Across the River and into the Trees* — all these (and many others who might also be cited) are men of a certain high kind of chivalry and of a most rigorous honesty, men who do not funk out in the moment of peril, who bear pain with reticence and dignity, who do not whine when defeated: and whatever it is that they do — whether it be bullfighting or fishing or prizefighting or hunting lions in the African bush or blowing up bridges as a military saboteur — is done with consummate skill and with pride of craft. These are men indeed who "carry" themselves in a way that bespeaks the high regard that they have for simplicity of life and precision of speech and consistency of conduct: they are tough and competent: they can be counted on in a tight squeeze, and they do not cheat or squeal or flinch at the prospect of danger, for in them conscience — at least through certain limited ranges of moral experience — is developed to a very fine point. In short, they have what Hemingway liked to speak of as *cojones* — which, without resort to euphemism, may be very simply translated as "guts."

But then — opposed to the Rinaldis and the Jordans and the Santiagos — there are the messy people, the people who have never learned how to behave with decency and dignity, or with a modicum of competence; and there is a large gallery of these anti-heroes in the novels and stories. One thinks, for example, of the Mr. Johnson in *To Have and Have Not* who engages Harry Morgan over several days to take him out in Morgan's boat to fish the stream off the Havana coast. Throughout much of this time he sulks because nothing is caught. But

25

then at last, on the eighteenth day, he hooks and fights and, through his own carelessness and stupidity and clumsiness, loses a great black marlin. And not only does he lose the fish but he also loses Morgan's gear, the rod and reel and line, worth nearly four hundred dollars. But, having made a fool of himself, instead of simply settling his bill and calling it quits, he stingily boggles at reimbursing Morgan for the lost tackle. Finally, though, they do, with much grumbling on Johnson's part, agree to a total figure covering eighteen days out on the stream and the lost gear, and Johnson promises, after docking and going to a bank, to return with the money — but, instead, he catches a plane for Miami and absconds.

Or, again, the portrayal of Robert Cohn in *The Sun Also Rises* makes another study in bad form. Cohn is a fawning, bathetic oaf who is filled with self-pity because of Brett's refusal of his love and who wants all his friends to know how painfully hurt he is by his chosen lady's rejection of him. And, in the design of the novel, the messiness of Cohn is beautifully juxtaposed against the splendidly integral and unpretentious manliness of the young matador, Pedro Romero, whose incorruptible simplicity is offered, presumably, as an example of the kind of strength and dignity that are achievable in the carefully codified life. In Hemingway's mythology, it is, of course, the bull ring where, of all places, a man is least able to get away with faking and where, as he stands exposed to the immediate threat of violent death, his stuff is put to the crucial test and is revealed as either genuine or false. And here is his description of Romero's style: he says:

> Romero never made any contortions, always it was straight and pure and natural in line. The others twisted themselves like corkscrews, their elbows raised, and leaned against the flanks of the bull after his horns had passed, to give a faked look of danger. Afterward, all that was faked turned bad and gave an unpleasant feeling. Romero's bull-fighting gave real emotion, because he kept the absolute purity of line in his movements and always quietly and calmly let the horns pass him close each time. He did not have to emphasize their closeness. . . . Since the death of Joselito all the bull-fighters had been developing a technic that stimulated this appearance of danger in order to give a fake emotional feeling, while the bull-fighter was really safe. Romero had the old thing, the holding of his purity of line through the maximum of exposure. . . .

26

It is a wonderfully appealing picture that is drawn, of probity and honor and good faith. And one feels that, for Hemingway, Romero is an example of something finer and more important even than rectitude in the bullring — that, in the completeness with which this young matador's manhood has been steeled by a difficult and dangerous discipline, we are expected to behold an image of that by which we can alone hope to resist the subversive power of Nada. Indeed, it is to be remarked that, in his encounter with the young Spaniard, Cohn is utterly bested. He discovers that the boy is sleeping with Brett and goes to his room to thrash him — which he is able easily to do, having become a skillful boxer as a Princeton undergraduate. But, though he knocks the matador down repeatedly, Romero each time gets up without uttering a single cry of pain, until Cohn himself is finally routed by the boy's stamina and begins to weep. Cohn knows, in other words, how to handle his fists: but, here, he is pitted against a deeper strength: so he caves in and makes the "bad show" of himself which, according to Hemingway's lesson, is to be expected of the undisciplined man. " 'That's quite a kid,' " says Bill Gorton — to which Mike Campbell replies: " 'He ruined Cohn.' "

Or, still again, if we turn to the collection of Hemingway's stories that appeared in 1938 (*The Fifth Column and the First Forty-Nine Stories*), we may find in "The Short Happy Life of Francis Macomber" yet another example of the "ruined" man, of the man who, having failed to internalize within himself an exacting standard of honor, inevitably caves in under the pressure of the slightest adversity. There does, of course, finally come a time when this young American sportsman, Francis Macomber, appears to have won the necessary virtues, under the guidance of the hunter Wilson; but, throughout most of the story, he is constantly failing all the crucial tests. He is a man of wealth who has been able to acquire a fashionable wife, but, in their relation, he is without any authority, and his wife does not, therefore, trouble to conceal either her sexual infidelity or her contempt for his lack of force. And, as the story opens, Macomber has "just shown himself, very publicly, to be a coward": in a hunting expedition on the Tanganyika plains, he has run away from a charging lion, and, as Wilson explains, this is something that one simply does not do — "You know in

Africa . . . no white man ever bolts." And not only has he turned heel and fled in panic but, on returning to their camp, he makes things even messier by apologizing and by asking Wilson not to tell anyone about the incident. "Now what in hell were you going to do about a man who talked like that," Wilson wonders, as he thinks about the whole episode which "had been about as bad as they come."

Nor is this the end of Macomber's indiscretions. For, on the next morning, another lion is tracked down, and, after being hit by a shot of Macomber's, it runs back into the tall grass. Now, of course, this last stage of the hunt is an exceedingly tricky and dangerous business, for, as Wilson says, in the appraisal of things that he gives to Macomber, " 'You can drive an unwounded lion — he'll move on ahead of a noise — but a wounded lion's going to charge. You can't see him until you're right on him. He'll make himself perfectly flat in cover you wouldn't think would hide a hare. . . . Somebody bound to get mauled.' " And, indeed, Macomber would very much like to avoid the encounter. So he proposes that the native "boys" be sent in after the beast. But Wilson has to remind him that they are not adequately armed for this "sort of a show," that to send them in would in effect be to slaughter them. And so Macomber proposes that the lion, then, be simply left in the grass — which immediately makes Wilson feel "as though he had opened the wrong door in a hotel and seen something shameful." And he has to explain to Macomber that they cannot merely pretend that the animal has not been hit, for they know that it is wounded and is therefore suffering: so it is unthinkable that they should simply walk away to leave it to die only after protracted agony. And, furthermore, were the lion to be left in the grass, someone else might run onto it unawares. Thus it is that he forces him to realize that there is nothing left to do but to go in and finish the job. But, then, when they do finally track the beast down, Macomber loses his nerve and bolts in panic, leaving Wilson to kill the charging animal.

Now, to be sure, Macomber does eventually learn how to behave with courage and honor in an extreme situation. On the following day they are hunting buffalo, and all at once he is no longer afraid: he hits a buffalo and can barely wait to go in-

28

to the grass after it: the excitement and the danger now bring the good thing, the great wonderful thrill of the hunt: it is, Hemingway explains, the "sudden precipitation into action without opportunity for worrying beforehand" that brings this about with Macomber. Now the fear is "gone like an operation. Something else grew in its place. . . . Made him into a man. . . . No bloody fear." But his "happy life" is short, for, when he goes in after the buffalo, his wife shatters his skull with a shot ostensibly aimed at the charging beast but aimed unconsciously, one suspects, at Francis, whose sudden access to manhood this woman (with her own real need for the kind of husband she has had) finds insupportable. Yet, even so — as Cleanth Brooks remarks of the story (in *The Hidden God*), in a marvelous act of recollection of an eighteenth-century poem — "One crowded hour of glorious life/Is worth an age without a name."

So there is a glory in the world that is rendered in Hemingway's fiction, a glory that helps Robert Jordan to die well in the Guadarrama mountains, that restores a lightness of heart to Nick Adams in the north woods of Michigan, that fills old Santiago with a reverential amazement at how beautiful and wondrous are the creatures of the sea and the sky. And it is a glory that establishes a certain *pietas* as one of man's principal obligations. But, besides the glory, there is a blackness, too — and a blackness that makes it necessary that a man's life be collected and deepened and concentrated through an unrelenting adherence to certain rigorous disciplines, disciplines that a Santiago has mastered and that a Francis Macomber has most painfully to learn before he can enter into his full human inheritance and escape the judgment that is carried in the thrust of Alexander Pope's line, "Never blessed, but always to be blessed."

Now it is in his first major novel, the book of 1926 — *The Sun Also Rises* — that we find Hemingway already bringing together what are for him the two sides of the essential truth about human existence, namely, the glory and the blackness. This is, of course, the book which, more than any other single literary work of its period, established — with the help of its epigraph from Gertrude Stein — the "lost generation" of the 'twenties as an abiding cultural fact of modern history. Its background is the American experience of the War of 1918 and of its aftermath of disillusionment — with the swollen rhetoric of duplicitous statesmen and with the inertia of established power. The novel finds its center in all those sad young people whom Scott Fitzgerald called "the beautiful and the damned," and it takes us down into the unhappy world of their expatriated life in "the condemned playground" of Europe in the mid-'twenties, where they languish amidst the ruins of faith and hope, stricken in their soured romanticism and astonished dispossession.

Jake Barnes is a young American newspaperman working in Paris, but working only just enough to be able to afford to eat and drink well and to travel about the Continent on fishing trips and excursions to bullfights. He is in love with the beautiful Lady Brett Ashley, but nothing can come of this, for he was rendered impotent by wounds suffered on the Italian front during the War. So Brett, though keeping her affection for Jake — " 'Oh, Jake, we could have had such a damn good time together' " — drifts from one casual affair to another. And she is the center of a group that is formed by Jake Barnes and the dissolute Scotsman Mike Campbell and the writer Bill Gorton and the ex-Princeton athlete and patron of literary causes, Robert Cohn. But Cohn is in this circle and yet not really of it, for his voluble and lugubrious emotionality excludes him from the freemasonry of those who cultivate the stoical virtues of clipped speech and controlled feeling and brisk insouciance; and, though there comes a time when he gives a brutal thrashing with his fists to a young matador in Pamplona, he is himself constantly being verbally thrashed by Mike Campbell, who in this expresses the mild contempt that is generally felt for Cohn in the circle of his Paris associates. These are all people charming in a small way, but aimless: it is a group — in and out of which others move from time to time — terribly dislocated by the whole war experience, moving like a wind that "goeth toward the south, and turneth about unto the north," whirling continually, from pillar to post. " 'Everybody's sick,' " says a little tart to Jake one night in a Paris hansom. And indeed the novel does very much appear to be spanning an awful darkness of the soul which makes the very experience of one's identity primarily — to take a phrase of Wilbur Frohock's about the book — an affair of "a ceaseless, dull ache."

But there is something else in the novel besides the blackness of disappointment and dereliction, besides all the bitter things that are made up of blasted hopes and closed futures: as Carlos Baker says, "Something tarnished is opposed to something bright." And it is after the scene of the novel shifts from the cafés and boulevards of Paris to the fiesta at Pamplona that we begin to see this bright thing, and to see that all may not be vanity of vanities and vexation of spirit. This section of the book brings a great intensification of pitch: the *aficionados* from Paris — Brett and Mike and Jake and Cohn — are quickly swept up into the frenzied gaiety of the fiesta, and all the tumultuous flurry of this wild frolic makes for something powerfully symbolic of the scrambled muddle of life represented by the revelers themselves. Yet there is something else which is presented in the Spanish section of the book. For one thing, there is the young matador, Pedro Romero, who, in the design of the novel's morality, exemplifies a kind of human order which one cannot help but feel to be a basic norm by which the Ashley-Campbell-Cohn axis of things is judged and found wanting: his "purity of line" and his holding of it "through the maximum of exposure" makes a sort of bar — a bar of judgment — before which the nymphomania of Brett and the undisciplined self-indulgence of Campbell and Cohn are brought for a very stringent assessment. But, then, beyond the polemical energy that, through Romero, the novel takes on vis-à-vis these hollow wastrels, there is something even more radically affirmative in the second main movement of the story (i.e., in the Spanish section) — and this is, I think, to be located in the Burguete episode.

Just before meeting Brett and Campbell and Cohn in Pamplona for the bullfights, Jake Barnes and Bill Gorton spend five days at an inn in the little hamlet of Burguete in the Pyrenees, from thence they walk out into the surrounding countryside each day to fish the streams in the Irati valley. And here the old "ceaseless, dull ache" of the Parisian world is put behind. High up in the mountains, the air is crisp and clean, and these two good friends exchange a "smile of complicity" with the clear trout streams and the golden Basque uplands, as they fish and enjoy their simple lunches of sandwiches and hardboiled eggs and wine. The frenetic neuroticism of Brett and her crowd is far away: indeed, Jake, as narrator, is careful to tell us that there is "no word from Robert Cohn nor from Brett and Mike." And we feel that he and Bill, with their lively raillery together and their quiet games of three-handed bridge at the inn in the evenings with the Englishman Wilson-Harris, are at last (like Nick Adams in "Big Two-Hearted River") *in the good place* — in a place, that is, where they can be touched by the good earth and its glory, by beech woods dense with old trees and foliage "thick but . . . not gloomy," by the running of rivers in valleys and the rising of the sun, by the bracing air of a mountain district and its untraveled sandy roads. And it is significant that, in his epigraph from Ecclesiastes, Hemingway speaks of how "the earth abideth forever."

During this whole movement of the narrative, all the tensions of the story are relaxed, and a great peace and calm settle over the novel. These five days at Burguete make, to be sure, but a brief season of tranquillity, and, as Jake and Bill move on to the frenzied festivities in Pamplona, the lovely stillness of the episode in the Pyrenees is soon drowned out by all the agitated dissonances with which the novel began. But, nevertheless, there is this serene and happy time, however brief, in which we are shown the power of a glory to dispel the black distempers which destroy man's peace — the glory which, as Wordsworth says, restores

> . . . . that blessed mood
> In which the burthen of the mystery,
> In which the heavy and the weary weight
> Of all this unintelligible world,
> Is lightened. . . .

Now, in relation to that dimension of things involving a "blackness, ten times black," I have stressed the Stoic *apatheia* which Hemingway believed it to be necessary for a man to summon, through the careful cultivation of a kind of martial poise and fortitude. But it remains to be remarked that it was not in this way alone that he felt the darkness beyond the campfire was to be staved off. For he seems also to have been deeply drawn towards something like the position of Matthew Arnold in "Dover Beach," that our "darkling plain" needs to prompt such a resolution as is expressed in the poignant cry uttered by Arnold's poem —

> Ah, love, let us be true
> To one another!

And it is in *A Farewell to Arms* (1929) that we get the first major expression of this religion of love. Robert Penn Warren, with his characteristic perceptiveness, speaks of the book indeed as "a religious book; if it does not offer a religious solution it is nevertheless," he says, "conditioned by the religious problem." And Hemingway's own inclination (reported by Edmund Wilson in *The Wound and the Bow*) to regard the novel as his *Romeo and Juliet* provides a kind of authorial sanction for our conceiving the book to be poised towards something like the kind of emphasis running through that tradition of courtly passion which is so masterfully (and hostilely) scanned in Denis de Rougemont's *Passion et L'Occident*.

The love story that is told about Catherine Barkley and Frederick Henry is not, however, an affair of an isolated duet, for we see, as Penn Warren says, "the figures of the lovers silhouetted against the flame-streaked blackness of war, of a collapsing world, of nada." It may have been some initial idealistic impulse to participate in the struggle to Make the World Safe for Democracy that carried the young American into the War of 1918 as a volunteer and into the medical corps of the Italian army, but there comes a time when the early idealism is corroded utterly by his shaken confidence in the worth of the society for which the struggle is being made and his revulsion by the terrible cost of human suffering exacted by modern warfare: there comes a time when to this young man it does indeed seem that the world hath neither

> . . . certitude, nor peace, nor help for pain;
> And we are here as on a darkling plain
> Swept with confused alarms of struggle and flight,
> Where ignorant armies clash by night.

The external sign of the general breakdown is the rain that seems everywhere and all the while to be falling along the Italian front: things are grinding to a halt, and disorder is rampant. So, after the Italian retreat from Caporetto, Frederick Henry (like Nick Adams) makes "a separate peace" and heads for the town where Catherine Barkley is living, the young English nurse with whom he had fallen in love while interned under her care in a hospital in Milan. And they escape into the Swiss Alps — where, only then, as Carlos Baker has noticed, "are they really out of the rain," in the chalet which they rent above Montreux.

And, as if to emphasize what it really is that these two have together, Hemingway arranges a conversation between Frederick and the old Count Greffi late one afternoon in Frederick's hotel at Stresa, just before he and Catherine leave for Switzerland. The two sip champagne, as they have a game of billiards together in the hotel's billiard-room, and, when the old man speaks of having read H. G. Well's novel *Mr. Britling Sees It Through* and of having thought it " ' a very good study of the English middle-class soul,' " Frederick replies: " 'I don't know about the soul.' " " 'Poor boy,' " says the Count: " 'We none of us know about the soul. Are you *Croyant?'* " And Frederick says: " 'At night.' " Which leads the old man to speak in tones of regret about his having failed somehow himself to become more devout as his life has lengthened out over the years. And he talks about the difficulties of old age, and they talk about the war — and then, as they are about to leave each other, he asks Frederick to pray for him, whenever it may be that Frederick becomes more devout, if he (the Count) is dead. Frederick promises that he shall, whatever may be the condition of his own faith. And their conversation concludes in this wise: first the Count says:

> "I had always expected to become devout. All my family died very devout. But somehow it does not come."
>
> "It's too early."
>
> "Maybe it is too late. Perhaps I have outlived my religious feeling."
>
> "My own comes only at night."
>
> "Then too you are in love. Do not forget that is a religious feeling."
>
> "You believe so?"
>
> "Of course."

Now it is indeed a precise statement of things that the old Count gives us, for the otherwise unemployed religious feelings of Catherine and Frederick are in fact engaged by their relation with each other — which is itself for them a waft of Grace. And thus the sweetness and beatitude of it need no ratification in marriage. For, as Catherine says to Frederick: " 'We are married privately . . . . You're my religion.' " And had such rhetoric been naturally congenial to her, she might also, one imagines, have reminded her beloved that "in Heaven there is neither marrying nor giving in marriage." They are, in short, these two (in Coventry Patmore's phrase), "Priest and Priestess to each other" of the Glory, and in their love itself they find *the good place* which offers shelter against all the dilapidation of a war-torn world and which establishes them in a heavenly City. Nor is this a City whose foundations are utterly crumbled by the fact that Catherine dies in childbirth: the disappearance of the Beatrician image does not invalidate the things that were done and said and enjoyed under its influence. And though, under the stress of his loss and grief, Frederick is crushed by a sense of nothing being able to escape the world's destructiveness, not even what he and Catherine have had together, in an earlier and happier time he had himself declared to her that "nothing ever happens to the brave."

The novel of 1937, *To Have and Have Not,* is an inconsequential fiction that Hemingway patched together out of a series of *Cosmopolitan* and *Esquire* stories about a Key West buccaneer on his uppers in the midst of the Depression, and it is his least satisfactory book (if one disregards, that is, *The Torrents of Spring).* In *The Green Hills of Africa,* which had appeared just two years earlier, in 1935, he had very explicitly set down his strong disinclination to be encumbered by any major social and political commitments: "If you serve time for society, democracy, and the other things quite young, and declining any further enlistment make yourself responsible only to yourself, you exchange the pleasant, comforting stench of comrades for something you can never feel in any other way than by yourself." Yet, even as he wrote these lines, there was being borne in upon him, ever more distressingly, a sense of the terrible pathos presented by the human dislocations arising out of the economic stoppages and large-scale unemployment of the early 'thirties. He had at this time for several years been living in Key West and was familiar with the work camps into which hundreds of unemployed veterans were herded on the Upper and Lower Matecumbe Keys, and he knew something of the despair that had taken hold of such people. So, despite his renunciation of social-political involvement in the book of 1935, he began to be moved by a great sympathy for the poor and for their helpless exposure to the irrational workings of economic life in an advanced technocratic culture. And the result was the chronicling in *To Have and Have Not* of the misfortunes of Harry Morgan, a Key West operator of a charter-boat, who wants only to make a decent provision for his wife and daughters and who, as a consequence of the economic slump, in order to earn a few dollars, is forced to engage in an enterprise of illegal smugglings that finally costs him his life. But the crudities of ideology (the Rich vs. the Poor; the System vs. the Underdog; the Haves vs. the Have-nots) and the snarled confusions of craft in *To Have and Have Not* reveal what might easily have been foreseen, that the métier of Dos Passos was not the métier of Hemingway.

Nor does that marvelous book of 1940, *For Whom the Bell Tolls,* have the effect of asserting the contrary. This account of three days in the life of an American volunteer attached to the Republican forces in the Spanish War entails the most elaborately plotted narrative that Hemingway ever attempted, and it is, I think — in the rich complexity of its structure, in the powerfully moving presentment of its major personages, in the beautiful gravity and stateliness of its language, in the boldly operatic accent of its melodramatism — one of the most brilliantly written novels of our time. But the book hardly lends itself to analysis in terms of such perspectives as are felt to be appropriate to works like Malraux's *Man's Fate* and Silone's *Bread and Wine* and Koestler's *Darkness at Noon.* Its ostensible subject, to be sure, is a crisis of politics and a revolutionary action. Yet if one thinks of the novel in relation, say, to such a book as George Orwell's *Homage to Catalonia,* one cannot help but feel how superficially it records what was involved — politically and humanly — in the Spanish War. The book does, of course, breathe a passionately felt sympathy for the Loyalist cause and an equally deep sense of chagrin at the tragic mischief practiced upon the

Spanish people by the Fascist movement, and its many various vignettes of isolated moments of the action — of guerrilla fighting and of the great confusion in the villages and of the new *fraternité* bred by the struggle — are often realized in a wonderfully living way. But the inchoateness with which the central issues of ideology and politics are defined may perhaps be taken as an index of how marginally in fact they stand with respect to Hemingway's most essential subject — which is, I believe, not a situation of revolutionary politics but the love story enacted by Maria and Robert Jordan. And, here, the emphasis is very much like that in *A Farewell to Arms*: it is on what Maria calls *la gloria* that the lovers are in together, and on its capacity to redeem and transfigure our human time, however filled it may be with tragic disappointment and however brief may be its span. La Gloria: it is, Jordan thinks, as he and Maria lie side by side on their last night, "the thing that is in the Cante Hondo and in the Saetas. . . . in Greco and in San Juan de la Cruz . . . ." And, though he and the girl have only three days, it is, nevertheless, *la gloria* which convinces them that "it is possible to live as full a life in seventy hours as in seventy years": and thus they know that neither death, nor life, nor angels, nor principalities, nor powers, nor things present, nor things to come can do any final kind of harm to what they have together: "they knew that nothing could ever happen to the one that did not happen to the other, that no other thing could happen more than this; that this was all and always . . . . Now and forever now . . . . not anything else only this now" — the Now of translation into Glory by the passionate intensity of "true love."

Hemingway's long silence after the appearance of *For Whom the Bell Tolls* was not broken until the publication a decade later of *Across the River and into the Trees*. That stiff-lipped, disciplined stoic whom we meet in Frederick Henry and Harry Morgan and Robert Jordan is now a man broken by the distempers of physical exhaustion, afflicted with high blood-pressure and cardiac disease, carrying about nitroglycerine pills in his pocket, and, like Stonewall Jackson in his last days, about to "cross the river and rest under the shade of the trees." And, in the story of Richard Cantwell, a colonel of the American army in postwar Venice for duck-shooting and to see his young mistress, it was, it seems, a kind of elegiac poem on the final terror and solitude of old age that Hemingway wanted to write. But, somehow, it was the Hemingway of the Legend who managed momentarily to win control of things, so that (as Philip Young remarks) it appears that "the unintentional delusion under which Hemingway labors throughout the novel is that he is being interviewed." The various characters "act as straight men, setting up implausible questions so that Cantwell can pontificate. When obliging reporters are not about, Hemingway interviews himself." And the result was a very poor performance indeed which ludicrously parodies the "vintage"-work, and with (what was for this novelist) a strange new kind of flaccid garrulity.

But "Papa" (as by now he had come very widely to be called by his friends and acquaintances) had, on his own testimony, "started out very quiet" and managed to beat "Mr. Turgenev": then he "trained hard and . . . beat Mr. de Maupassant" — after which he had "fought two draws with Mr. Stendhal," yet all the while retaining a modest determination not "to get . . . in any ring with Mr. Tolstoy unless I'm crazy or I keep getting better." And his friend John O'Hara was able (in his *New York Times* review) to find evidence even in *Across the River and into the Trees* of his being the greatest writer since Shakespeare — "the outstanding author out of the millions of writers who had lived since 1616." So, however much these comparisons may have been somewhat askew, it was perhaps unwise in 1950 to take it for granted, as many did, that this talent was irredeemably spent. And the unwisdom of this was indeed most emphatically demonstrated just two years later by the last novel, *The Old Man and the Sea,* whose formal immaculateness and whose austere eloquence place it unquestionably amongst such absolute masterpieces of the twentieth century as Kafka's *The Trial* and Conrad's *The Secret Agent* and Stevens's *Harmonium* and Eliot's *Quartets* and Beckett's *Waiting for Godot.*

In this superbly executed tragic novella and its magnificently simple story of an old fisherman's stamina before the assaults and vicissitudes of the sea, we have what is undoubtedly Hemingway's finest image of the human voyager. Though Santiago does not succeed in bringing his great marlin back to the shore, he does, nevertheless, in the great invincibility of his fortitude, hurl back at the massive indifference of the world a kind of promise, a kind of guaranty, that man shall ultimately prevail: and thus he emerges triumphant, the parable offering the example of his heroism as an example of that in the strength of which is to be rested whatever confidence can be summoned that we shall finally survive the difficulties of this life, unimpaired. The old mariner has fished "far out," because it is what "he was born for"; and, though he loses his prize, he fishes well: he does not betray the disciplines of his trade: nor does he betray the spiritual disciplines by which his humanity has been formed. For, at the end, even in his exhaustion and defeat, there is no wheedling querulousness, no petulant indulgence in self-pity, only the poised and self-contained dignity of a man who has done all that he could do when that was what he found to be required. And thus Santiago's voyage is that which, sooner or later, is destined for Everyman. This is Hemingway's final testament.

And to this last testament the posthumous book of 1964, *A Moveable Feast,* may be considered a sort of postscript. It is a beautifully written account of his life in the city of Paris in the years between 1921 and 1926, the memoir itself having been composed in the period between the autumn of 1957 and the spring of 1960. And the book, in the record it affords of personal relationships and experience, is drenched in love (of Paris, of his young wife Hadley Richardson, of his friends Ezra Pound, Sylvia Beach, William Bird) and in malice (toward Gertrude Stein and Ford Madox Ford and Scott Fitzgerald and various others) — but drenched, above all else, in happiness, in the happiness of a young man who, in the early 'twenties, having thrown over his newspaper work, was getting under way what was destined to be — along with Joyce's and Faulkner's — one of the great careers among the novelists of this century.

Now we have looked at the full stretch of Hemingway's life in literature. And we have reviewed the principal "ideas" which are at the center of that life — the sense of the consolatory and redemptive glory of the earth, the consequent sense of a certain *pietas* as forming one of man's principal obligations; then the blackness, the *nada,* the nothingness, which contradicts the glory, and the consequent necessity both for the artist and the human being of steeling oneself against chaos through rigorous and austere disciplines of mind and spirit; and, finally, the dream of the possibility of transcendence — through love: a kind of minimalist "theology of romantic love." These are the basic "ideas" that stir the fiction into life, and those readers who are disposed to take a bilious view of it will tell us no doubt that these are ideas which at best comprise "a confection of synthetic wisdom" (the phrase is Irving Howe's) and a quite unremarkable "philosophy." I suspect, however, that something like this will appear to be true of the "ideas" that figure in much of the greatest literature in the tradition, once they are violently submitted to discursive systematization. I also suspect that the originality and importance of the artist are to be judged not by his ideas as such but by the dramatic use he puts them to. And, when the appraisal is made on this level, there is surely no difficulty that need be encountered in maintaining that, however much limitation and poverty may be a part of his basic ideas, Hemingway managed, out of those ideas, to create one of the most haunting bodies of fiction in the literature of our time.

It is, of course, a fiction from which much is left out — entire ranges of feeling, of behavior, of society and politics. Yet, despite the narrowness of its intensity, Hemingway's is a vision that has had a powerfully gripping effect on the modern imagination — and, I would say, (at least in large part) because of what has been felt to be its essentially religious seriousness. Indeed, I would go so far even as to say that, in very nearly quite the precise sense in which the term is used in Catholic theology, he was, at bottom, a "spiritual writer," for the drama being enacted just beneath the clenched surfaces of his fiction is that of the soul's journey in search of God.

To speak in this way is, of course, quite probably to cause a wince of irritation in many secular circles, for none are more fastidious about what is (and is not) to be accorded status amongst things religious than they for whom the issues of religion are of no real account at all. In matters of religious discrimination, theirs is a sense of the proprieties whose impeccableness would often seem to put the orthodox to shame. And when, say, a Christian interpreter of culture discerns evidences

40

of the residual presence of religious forms and concerns in some body of modern literature that announces itself as radically secular, when he detects in this body of poetry or in that body of drama phases of Christian thought and feeling that have, as it were, gone underground and taken on strange new accents and guises, he will be quickly written off by many of his agnostic colleagues in the critical forum as being a "religionist" who simply hopes to shore up and win prestige for his religiosity by becoming a fellow-traveler of what is modish and *au courant*. He will be told either that he is a fool or, even worse, that, intellectually, he represents downright dishonesty, and that what is nothing more than a silly kind of connoisseurship of *seriousness* he allows to betray him into making *seriousness* itself, wherever it may be found, something that is "for" the Christian faith. No, he will be told, you do not have anything Christian, except where you have explicit reliance on a particular tradition of Christian orthodoxy, on its symbolism and conceptual structures and cultic forms and all its protocol. So it is that a very familiar form of heckling goes. But I cannot myself put down the suspicion that this is a fastidiousness which, as it is sometimes expressed by secular intellectuals today, is chiefly prompted by a desire very tightly to segregate — and thus to expel — Christianity from the general community of culture. For the fact of the matter is that the Christian faith has ceased to be something unambiguous and pristine, whenever it has entered into alliance with a cultural enterprise — even in Dante, even in Milton, to say nothing of such equivocal moderns as Hawthorne and Baudelaire and Joyce and Simone Weil. Indeed, it ought to be regarded as one of the great lessons of the Incarnation that a faith which is grounded in a Divine act of self-*emptying (kenosis)* will itself always be, as it were, an affair of Diaspora — dying in order to live, wedding itself (as Amos Wilder says, in *Modern Poetry and the Christian Tradition)* to changing forms and sensibilities "in a daring surrender of life, and [thus introducing] creative energies and perspectives which then make their appearance in secular form," and in ways undistinguished by any evangelical stamp.

So I have no great hesitancy at all in speaking of Hemingway as a "spiritual writer," and I suspect that Carlos Baker is more right than wrong in declaring that "the consciousness of God is in his books." Secular guardians of Christian integrity, armed as they are with their Baedekers of theological rectitude, will no doubt boggle at this, but, nevertheless, something like Professor Baker's claim deserves to be made. For, however much (as Scholastic theologians would say) at the level of ontological knowledge and in the order of being it is Hemingway's tendency to make the testimony of nihilism, it is also his tendency, as I have tried to suggest, at the level of practical and affective knowledge, to keep a profound sense of the radical holiness of the world. Though his books admittedly — and obviously — express a sharp sense of the causality which is exercised in human existence by *nada,* by the absurd, by the power of blackness, they also express a sense of man as a creature who is, willy-nilly, the *homo religiosus* — moved by intimations of the Sacred, and searching his experience for a principle whereby what is "felt along the heart" may be validated, despite (in Wordsworth's phrase) "the uneasy thoughts which [fill the] mind": it is very much like what one would expect to be the vision of a "spiritual writer" who is thoroughly of this present time.

And not only does the fiction suggest the impropriety of attributing to Hemingway a position of simple and undialectical nihilism at the level of *metaphysics,* but so too does it also suggest how manifestly such a judgment would be wrong at the level of the *morality* of his stories and novels. For, here, as I have emphasized, what is most noticeable is the stringency of the discipline to which men are held accountable. And, in this dimension of things, it is customary to invoke the nomenclature (in the upper case) of Stoicism. Nor would I turn this usual procedure aside, for, though the relation of this modern vision to that of classical Greek and Roman Stoicism is far from being one of a point-for-point correspondence, the comparison does at least have the merit of calling attention to the indubitably Stoical quality of that *apatheia* which is very much of the essence of the particular human style which did for Hemingway best express the dignity of man. And, when the religious position of Hemingway is being measured, the comparison with Stoicism has also the merit of calling attention to the virtual excision altogether, at the level of the fiction's morality, of any vestige of the distinctively Christian sense of tragedy. The literature is, of course, impregnated by a profound tragic sense, but it is one that springs basically from a sense of the disproportionate odds by which man — in his creatureliness and finitude — is handicapped in his struggle with the intractabilities of his world-environment: the tragic sense in Hemingway is never anything that springs from such a sense of defeat as St. Paul expressed in his poignant cry, ". . . the good that I would I do not: but the evil which I would not, that I do." When there is despair in the fiction, it is never a despair that springs from a sense of anything unreliable or defective in the human heart itself, and Hemingway is never prepared to say, with Hamlet, that "conscience" doth make cowards of us all. For like Epictetus and Seneca and the great Stoics generally, though he believed the indispensable human virtue to be the virtue of courage, he seems not to have had any deep sense of our needing to find a courage that permits us to deal with the reality and power of sin.

But let it be said in conclusion, though, that the man who produced *The Sun Also Rises* and *For Whom the Bell Tolls* and *The Old Man and the Sea* was a *good* Stoic. Though he found absurdity in the world, he never endorsed it, and kept always a profoundly reverential sense of the opposite possibility of glory too. Though he found that in the human voyage which might strike terror to the heart, he was never overwhelmed by it, and there is not even the merest breath of cynicism in his books. Nor was he ever deluded by the supposition that reality is manageable, that it can be brought to heel by dint of some mere formula of thought or action, for he knew that neither man nor the world is simple. And, finally, there is in his best work a power of love, there is a very moving kind of gentleness, which does, I suspect, in no small way constitute a part of his greatness. "In the equipment of the moralist," says Lionel Trilling, "and therefore in the equipment of the novelist, aggression plays an important part, and although it is of course sanctioned by the novelist's moral intention and by whatever truth of moral vision he may have, it is often none the less fierce and sometimes even cruel." But though Hemingway, as I have argued,

43

is to be seen in one phase of his work as having been consistently committed to the role of moralist, yet we feel of him, as Mr. Trilling remarks of Scott Fitzgerald, that

> . . . in his morality he was more drawn to celebrate the good than to denounce the bad. We feel of him, as we cannot feel of all moralists, that he did not attach himself to the good because this attachment would sanction his fierceness toward the bad — his first impulse was to love the good, and we know this the more surely because we perceive that he loved the good not only with his mind but also with his quick senses and his . . . pride and desire.

SELECTED BIBLIOGRAPHY

PRINCIPAL WORKS OF ERNEST HEMINGWAY

Three Stories and Ten Poems. Paris and Dijon: Contact Publishing Co., 1923.

In Our Time. New York: Boni and Liveright, 1925.

The Torrents of Spring. New York: Charles Scribner's Sons, 1926.

The Sun Also Rises. New York: Charles Scribner's Sons, 1926.

Men Without Women. New York: Charles Scribner's Sons, 1927.

A Farewell to Arms. New York: Charles Scribner's Sons, 1929.

Death in the Afternoon. New York: Charles Scribner's Sons, 1932.

Winner Take Nothing. New York: Charles Scribner's Sons, 1933.

The Green Hills of Africa. New York: Charles Scribner's Sons, 1935.

To Have and Have Not. New York: Charles Scribner's Sons, 1937.

The Fifth Column and the First Forty-Nine Stories. New York: Charles Scribner's Sons, 1938.

For Whom the Bell Tolls. New York: Charles Scribner's Sons, 1940.

Across the River and into the Trees. New York: Charles Scribner's Sons, 1950.

The Old Man and the Sea. New York: Charles Scribner's Sons, 1952.

A Moveable Feast. New York: Charles Scribner's Sons, 1964.

CURRENT AMERICAN REPRINTS

In Our Time. New York: Scribner Library.

The Sun Also Rises. New York: Scribner Library.

A Farewell to Arms. New York: Scribner Library.

The Green Hills of Africa. New York: Scribner Library.

For Whom the Bell Tolls. New York: Scribner Library.

The Old Man and the Sea. New York: Scribner Library.

The Snows of Kilimanjaro and Other Stories. New York: Scribner Library.

The Short Stories of Ernest Hemingway. New York: Modern Library.

The Hemingway Reader, ed. Charles Poore. New York: Scribner Library.

A Moveable Feast. New York: Bantam Books.

BIOGRAPHICAL STUDIES

Aronowitz, Alfred G. and Peter Hamill, *Ernest Hemingway: The Life and Death of a Man.* New York: Lancer Books, 1961.

Fenton, Charles A., *The Apprenticeship of Ernest Hemingway.* New York: Farrar, Straus and Young, 1954.

Hemingway, Leicester, *My Brother, Ernest Hemingway.* Cleveland and New York: World Publishing Co., 1962.

Hotchner, A. E., *Papa Hemingway*. New York: Random House, 1966.

Ross, Lillian, "How Do You Like It Now, Gentlemen?" *New Yorker*, 26:36-62 (May 13, 1950). Reprinted as *Portrait of Hemingway* (Harmondsworth, Middlesex: Penguin Books, 1962).

CRITICAL STUDIES

Baker, Carlos, *Hemingway: The Writer as Artist*. Princeton: Princeton University Press, 1956 (2nd ed.).

Baker, Carlos, ed., *Hemingway and His Critics: An International Anthology*. New York: Hill and Wang, 1961.

Killinger, John, *Hemingway and the Dead Gods*. Lexington: University of Kentucky Press, 1960.

McCaffery, John K., ed., *Ernest Hemingway: The Man and His Work*. Cleveland and New York: World Publishing Co., 1950.

Rovit, Earl H., *Ernest Hemingway*. New York: Twayne Publishers, 1963.

Sanderson, Stewart, *Hemingway*. Edinburgh: Oliver & Boyd, 1961.

Weeks, Robert Percy, ed., *Hemingway*. Englewood Cliffs, N.J.: Prentice-Hall, 1962.

Young, Philip, *Ernest Hemingway*. New York: Rinehart, 1952.

Young, Philip, *Ernest Hemingway*. Minneapolis: University of Minnesota Press, 1959. Number 1 in "University of Minnesota Pamphlets on American Writers."

> Note: The most comprehensive checklist of Hemingway criticism is to be found in Carlos Baker's anthology, *Hemingway and His Critics*.